A CORNISH YEAR IN POEMS AND PAINTINGS

This collection of work was put together as a celebration of life in Cornwall through its places, seasons, landscapes and festivals which mark the turning year. The poems and paintings were created as individual pieces but they also complement and reflect each other to create a dialogue between the two art forms.

A Cornish Year
by Frank Pickering and Wendy Parkyn

© Frank Pickering and Wendy Parkyn 2018

A catalogue card for this book is available from the British Library.

Hardback ISBN: 978-1-9999772-8-3

First published in 2018

Publication support
TJ INK
tjink.co.uk

Printed and bound in Great Britain by TJ International, Padstow, Cornwall

PAINTINGS

POEMS

JANUARY

"Degol Stuhl" is the Cornish celebration of 12th Night. A "Noz Lowen" (Happy Night) is a Cornish dance evening and echoes the Breton "Fez Noz".

PENRYN

DEGOL STUHL NOZ LOWEN

This boat-like room's inverted wooden V
Reflects the hulls that nod and creak outside
Against the lapping quay. The wind and rain
Which every day has driven us indoors
This winter season curses spite at our
Bold caterwauling, impotent to break
The wheeling rings and winding serpent coils
Or mute the fiddles and violas. Hand
In hand bold dancers trip from light to night,
The music fading to a dying fall.
A virtuous black-backed gull on yellow legs
Looks down from mast-top disapprovingly
And yarks contempt as we return inside
To warmth and light and music, cakes and ale.

FEBRUARY

This is what you get for living on the coast!

TREVONE

STORM

When the chimney howls
Like a hoover,
Windows glaze with salt
And foam soaps the fields
We brace for another assault
From the edge of the world.
A white fury
Scours the shore,
Bites chunks off the land
And rips away rocks.
Geysers punched skywards
Are smacked inland
By the driven air.
Waterfalls bend backwards
And break.
We cling like limpets,
Fearing the day our grip loosens
And the sea marches in triumph
Up the road.

FEBRUARY

TREVONE

GALE

Beaten hostile by the pelting dark
We walk the narrow shore with careful steps.
The sweeping water coldly plucks our legs,
Rehearsing for the long trip to the depths.
And suddenly all shelters are unsound,
Destruction hides no longer, fight we must,
We bare our teeth and stand our battleground
On blasting sand that scours us into dust.
If this were all, what heroes would emerge
From elements spectacularly staged,
What pride of strength to wrestle with the surge,
Outface all odds, defiantly enraged!
Not sapped by sickness, undermined by years,
Empoisoned by disgust, heart-sick with fears.

MARCH

There is a strong tradition of male voice choral singing in Cornwall.
The international festival draws choirs from across the world.

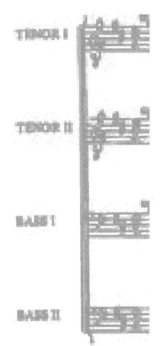

HALL FOR CORNWALL, TRURO

MALE VOICE CHOIR

In slacks and blazers from a bygone time
They file onstage, grey, ancient schoolboys, badged
By sticks, bifocals, dentures, crested ties,
The once firm steps become a shaky trudge.

And then a transformation. Richly layered,
Strong, certain voices draw from wells of youth
And overcome the stoops, the scanty hair,
Arthritic fingers and ill-fitting teeth

And what we see are not retired men –
Old farmers, bankers, plumbers, teachers, clerks,
Infilling unproductive days with songs
And dressing-up to mask their pains and aches

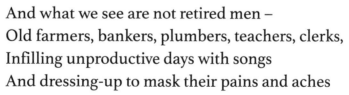
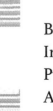

But virile lovers borne on passion's stream,
Intrepid soldiers boldly facing death,
Pure, blessed saints transfigured by faith's calm
And sages blending harmony with truth.

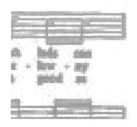

MARCH

The ties between Brittany and Cornwall are close both in language and culture. These are celebrated at an Easter event called "Aberfest" with dancing and singing in and around Falmouth.

FALMOUTH

COUSIN JACQUES

These Bretons who were Britons
Many lives ago,
Who fled with lore and language
Across the British Sea,
Peopled a land which once,
In unwatched times,
Conjoined their home.

Each spring they cross Mor Breizh
With bagpipe and with bombarde
From Finisterre to Land's End,
Cornouaille to Cornwall,
To sing the warmth of family
And dance the circles of time.

MARCH

March 6th is St Piran's Day and events which celebrate Cornish identity take place throughout the county. In Perranporth, where Piran is said to have arrived floating on a millstone, his effigy is brought from the sea and paraded through the town. This poem, like "Descent" looks at roots, differences and similarities.

PERRANPORTH

TRIBES

Our Sunday school banner
Was gloriously unlike its shabby chapel.
Scarlet, blue, and gold
With scrolls and tassels
It weighed a ton.
Hauled out each spring
And wrestled with ropes, like a square-rigger,
Through the streets and lanes of my northern village
We sang to flapping hymn sheets
And pitied outsiders.
We ended in some dusty room
Where doughty ladies wielded tea-pots
The size of watering cans
And there were potted-meat sandwiches
And lemon-curd tarts.

These faithless days
St Piran floats in by inflatable
For his cold march
In draughty Perranporth.
The tinners, bal-maidens, music and flags
Parade a black-and-white case of identity.
To which I cannot belong
But there will still be tea in some dusty room
And pasties and saffron cake.

APRIL

Richard Trevithick was born in Illogan and educated in Camborne. He grew to be six foot two inches and was known as the Cornish giant. His contribution to the industrial revolution and steam power in particular was immense. Trevithick Day is marked by a parade of steam vehicles of all kinds, including a full-sized replica of Trevithick's own "Puffing Devil".

CAMBORNE

TREVITHICK DAY

Working towns look uncomfortable
In holiday wear.
Behind the bright bunting,
Blunt terraces front the streets,
A sepia maze
Of faded industrial might
Built out of the land's granite heart
By its deep riches.

A dark, devout place
Which saw a giant harness a revolution
In hellish alchemy of fire and water
And, watched by the still horses,
Move the world.

On this day, above silent lodes,
Between the cars, crowds and cream-teas
There rumbles the tough remnants
Of that elemental age.
Built for toil,
They labour to entertain
Like melancholy elephants
Goin' up Camborne Hill
Comin' down.

19

MAY

"'Oss, 'oss, wee 'oss!" shout the crowds. Drum beats echo off the house walls and the May Day song threads the streets throughout the day. This ancient ceremony of rejuvenation and rebirth is unique and hypnotic.

PADSTOW

MAY DAY

A stubborn survivor,
This green sycamore branch
Has kept its spring
And flexed to the wrestle of time
Still singing simple truths
Of life and death.

Out of the white mouth
Of winter's cave
The old words waft.
From black galleries and tunnels,
Rubble-strewn, half-choked
Yet joined to ancient magic
Come echoes, whispers, a thread of melody.

A dance to defy the dark.
The clannish dervishes are unstabled
And whirl through the long day.
Teased like black bulls
They breathe misrule
And maypole potency,
Marking ground, uniting the steep streets.

At the centre
A bright heart drums.
Light is lived
In a frenzy of sense
Under the climbing sun
Between night song and farewell.

21

JUNE

In June, 2008, a festival was held to celebrate Cornwall's mining heritage. It was called "Smoking Chimneys" and engine houses around Carn Brea lit fires to send smoke up the chimneys as a reminder of what a thriving industrial landscape looked like.

CARN BREA

SPOIL

The hillside is pocked with waste,
Greened over like an old battlefield.
Quiet cattle nose now where once
Rich ore was ripped from the ground.
Each engine-house has its hand up
To signal the sites of silent shafts.
They breathe out coils of smoke
Recalling a time
When the valley rang with work
And the earth's bounty seemed endless.

JULY

There is a series of books called "Cornish Wrecks" and one has a map showing the sites of wrecks on the Doom Bar in the Camel estuary. In the days of sail it was a lethal hazard.

STEPPER POINT

DOOM BAR

At this, the lowest tide of the year
You can see me.
You may let your children shriek
And splash away their summer days
Along my muscled arm,
But remember, too, the lost sailors
Crying out on black winter nights
When I played hide-and-seek
For keeps.

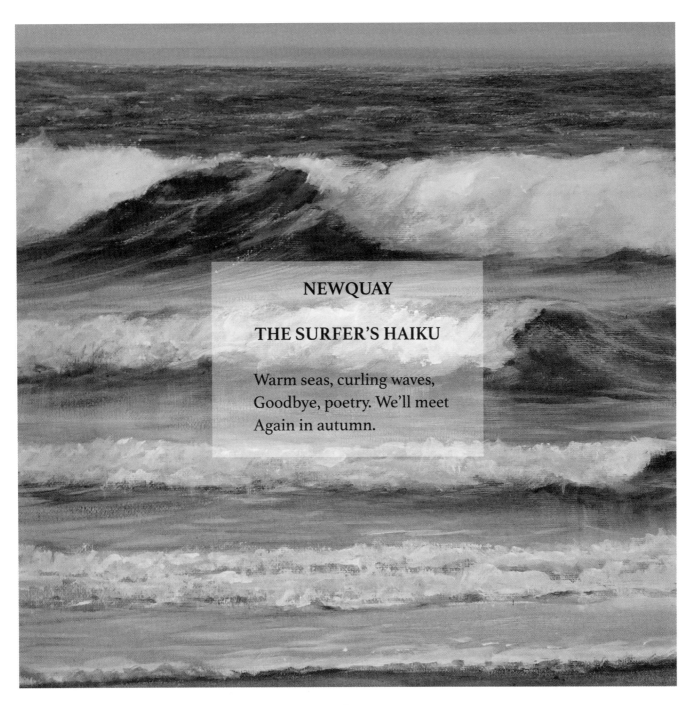

NEWQUAY

THE SURFER'S HAIKU

Warm seas, curling waves,
Goodbye, poetry. We'll meet
Again in autumn.

JULY

When you sit out back, waiting for a wave, you sometimes have leisure to watch and ponder. I got to thinking about evolution…

THE GREEN ROOM

In suspense we sit or lie
Cradled by a breathing sigh
Rocked between the earth and sky

Blennies blend to sea-bed lap
Silver sand-eels coil and flap
Wrasse leap, bright in rainbow wrap

Cormorants fly beneath the swells
Hawking terns scream fork-tailed yells
Mad-eyed gannets drop like shells

Our unfathomable ways
Draw the seals' astonished gaze
Dolphins deftly sew the waves

Rich ingredients combine
Evolution's fertile brine
No man's land and borderline

Rising up we firmly stand
Fin transformed to foot and hand
Dance our way from sea to land.

AUGUST

The story goes that a mermaid, in human guise, would occasionally join the church choir at Zennor church. She fell for a young chorister, Mathey Trewella ("the best singer in the parish") and enticed him to come away with her. Neither was seen again on dry land although she was seen again in mermaid form near Pendower Cove. The ancient carving on a bench end in Zennor church shows a very early image of a mermaid.

ZENNOR

THE MERMAID OF ZENNOR

Whilst white-haired combers rake Pendower Cove
And livid sun ignites the mirroring sea
You outwait centuries within the cool
And holy half-light of Senara's church,
Your passion spent, the blazing need, desire
And deadly craving, flooding tides of love,
All ebbed away, your image left behind
Like flotsam, enigmatic, dark and still.
When Lawrence drifted here in fiery love
With tangled life he brushed his hand across
These carved and confined tresses, chaos caught
And smoothed by craft, all complications gone.
My fingers follow his. I fear your fate,
Embracing sun and lovers and this life.

29

SEPTEMBER

As reminders of a brutal past, these buildings are the stuff of nightmares.

BODMIN

BODMIN GAOL

Shoved into the corner of the town
Like something shameful
It has the terrible architecture
Of a concentration camp.
The triumphant mouth
Swallows hope.
Sterile yards, like urban playgrounds
Are blank deserts with nowhere to hide.
Its hard heart is a gothic nightmare,
A cellular keep
For those who have become things.
The stern tower raises an admonishing finger.

Built out of fear,
To tame the ignorant and desperate
With silence, toil and pain.
It broke dangerous spirits on the wheel,
And left tormented souls to pick and pick.
Wild young men had their world

Yanked from under kicking feet,
A sixty-one minute turn
For an audience of pitiless authority
And gawping trainloads.
Colluding religion snatched easy souls
From the despair.

It stubbornly refuses to soften with time.
Stripped of its lead and slate
These brutal stones will not separate.
Cold even on the warmest day
The summer-clad visitor
Leaves with a shiver, feels sullied,
Uneasy at the picnic tables
By the execution shed.
The gallery brackets hang like gibbets
Above nettles and broken glass.
The air is tainted with misery,
The ground guilty with graves.

SEPTEMBER

This sonnet was inspired by the annual charity swim from Padstow to Rock.

THE CAMEL ESTUARY

HERO

When he let slip the land and shouldered through
The grey, face-slapping, sour, dishwater waves,
The estuary appeared to shudder, though
The tide was slack. This crossing pledged, he wove
A serpentine wake around mooring buoys
Out to the deep, so far from either shore
That had he begged the haven of a bay
Returning were as tedious as go o'er.
When near the prize, with spirit almost spent
He looked to see his pounding heart's desire.
He was Leander, this his Hellespont.
The landfall in retreat laughed from afar.
Hope ebbed before the fast-receding coast.
The tide had turned beneath him. He was lost.

OCTOBER

There are two curious maze patterns carved into the rock face in this beautiful rugged valley. They are believed to be about 4000 years old. Who were the people who made them? What was their purpose?

I wrote these words to a tune called "Mixkovals" by the Swedish band, "Groupa". The song is recorded on Caracana's CD "The Banks of the Fowey" (see www.caracana.info)

TINTAGEL

ROCKY VALLEY

The wind weaves patterns on the stones
And raindrops wear the land,
Softening, caressing
Waves cut caves into the shore
While valleys sink below streams

So time is traced into the land
Each rolling moment leaves
Witness to its passing
Read the story of the earth
As seasons follow in turn

Our sweet and fleeting lives too
Leave footprints palely pressing,
Echoes of our passing
Shapes and shadows fading fast
Fragments faintly fixed by fate

Let harmony be our gift
And music offer all that
Leads to happiness and
When the melody is gone
May we leave behind our love.

OCTOBER

A starlit sky is becoming a rare sight as we illuminate our world around the clock. Cornwall still has its precious pockets of darkness.

TREVONE

LIGHT YEARS

Every night our land
Becomes a fairground.
Seen from space
The clustered cities glister,
Constellations set against
The inconvenient dark.

Above us, not so far,
(About an hour's drive, if cars
Could only motor skywards) are
The infinite confines
Where past and future meet,
Brilliant depths
Which once we told
Like a clock,
Its familiar, cold comfort
Invisible now
Behind our shining stars.

OCTOBER

"The Saints' Way" is a walking trail of about 70 miles starting at Padstow Church and finishing at Fowey Church.

PADSTOW TO FOWEY

FORTH AN SYNS

The way to cross this long land
Foot by foot, from sea to sea,
Is routed in that quiet time
Of breeze and birdsong
Before we left the fields
And became citizens.
The path is mapped
In faded marks –
 Grassed mound, fallen stone,
Blurred cross and lichened well –
Where myth and matter mingle.
The wolves are long gone,
The busy inns are cottages again
But the way remains
For us to measure up
Against the earth
On a crossing that is blessed.

NOVEMBER

This song is my Cornish version of a traditional folk story. It occurs in various guises around the world. You can hear it as the title track on Caracana's CD "The Banks of the Fowey" (www.caracana.info)

RESPRYN

THE BANKS OF THE FOWEY

It was late in the evening as the autumn light fell
A stranger came wand'ring through wood, field and dell
To find ease for his heart-ache he'd roamed the wide world
And he found in the west land a sweet Cornish girl
She was graceful as the grasses that waved on the moor
She was bright as the waters that washed to the shore
And her hair was like a halo around her face furled
And he fell for the charms of that sweet Cornish girl

'Oh may I walk beside you on the banks of the Fowey
For you've captured the heart of this wandering boy
I could stay here forever with you by my side
And never more roam the cold world so wide'
She said, 'I'll walk beside you in Tristram's fair dells
And speak with you sweetly by these holy wells
But I'm bound to another who's far, far away
And I know he'll return for me some day'

He wrapped her in his arms where she clung like a child
And she wept for she knew that her heart was beguiled
By this stranger whose touch turned her body to flame
And her loving heart was riven in twain

'I must wait and be faithful, our love cannot be'
He said, 'I will go, you'll nevermore see'
As they vowed to each other they cried out in pain
For they knew they must never be parted again
So they walked to the river, hand in hand, side by side
Were embraced by the water, washed away by the tide
Round each other enfolding their arms tightly curled
Now he's kissing forever his sweet Cornish girl

When you hear the sweet curlew cry over the moors
Or the breeze whisper secrets across these high tors
When the wavelets lap gently against the long strand
It's a sigh for these lost lovers from this sweet land
By the green banks of Fowey where the wind shadows dart
You might hear in the ripples 'You've stolen my heart'
And then faint, his reply, 'Oh you're my precious pearl
And I love you; I love you, my sweet Cornish girl.

41

NOVEMBER

We know that terrible things happen all the time of which we are unaware. It seems important to recognise that good things happen too.

HAL'S GRAVE, WHITECROSS

REMEMBER, REMEMBER

One glance at the fuel gauge
And I rush past the dark garage
This cold, wet November night,
Warmly wrapped in instrument glow,
Driving home
To love, welcome, light.

In the grim house behind the pumps
Lies a murdered man, his corpse
Waiting to be discovered in
the light of pitiful day.
Shotgunned.
Outside, his wife, bludgeoned
To death as she tried to crawl away,

And I learn, when the news breaks
That they met their appalling fate
As I heedlessly, happily passed.
I think of Auden's "Musee des Beaux Arts"

And how Breughel's Icarus drowns
In a corner, unnoticed

By the indifferent ploughman, suffering
No distraction to the ship's busy sailing,
All furrows made in blindness.
But I know, too, that lives are quietly saved
At every moment, each second,
love is offered
Unregarded, like constant,
unpraised acts of kindness,

And for these reasons,
For all instinctive compassion,
Forgiveness given, mercy shown,
Want supplied, self-sacrifice made,
Uncelebrated, unthanked,
done for its own sake,
I still believe in goodness. That it does atone.

NOVEMBER

I wrote this poem after an end of season visit in 1969. I remember there was a sign outside a cafe which read, "No Beatniks".

ST IVES

Waves break the headland like cannon
Crashing their volleys, cracking rock,
Surge salt spray, fling wild water
Skywards hissing.
Stone harbour walls glisten wet
With rain and fret.
A gull perched on a chimney cowl
Lifts a webbed foot and ruffles his feathers.
The white-fronted houses soak
In boom and thunder.
Screams of seabirds, seaweed, smells.
Boats moored to rusty rings
Swirl to the incoming tide,
Bumping together.
The steeply-sided cove collects
Light, scent and sound
In a half-opened hand
And pushes it seawards.

DECEMBER

Trevarno estate near Helston used to have a herd of reindeer. That was enough to evoke Christmas.

TREVARNO

A CHRISTMAS CAROL

Reindeer in the rain
With pearls on their velvety antlers
Made a cool summer day dissolve.
I saw snow slant across shorn lawns,
Heard music melt in crystal rooms
And felt a close ghost of Christmas past
Take my hand and make me happy.

47

DECEMBER

I once sang in a Cornish choir and we performed Christmas concerts across the county. There was one stormy night in Mullion when you could taste salt in the air.

MULLION

CHRISTMASTIDE IN CORNWALL

This is the season
When the sea takes to the air,
Its salt breath
Sniffing out cracks
In the hunkered down houses.
Its blows
Whump and hiss
Against the groaning headlands
And broken-ribbed, flung beaches.

Here, time turns to a moony tug
Dragging this limb of land
In and out of the ocean.
Breath shallows and deepens
As the shores flood and ebb.

Deep down impossible lanes
Hidden hamlets with improbable names
Sing of the dusty east,
Of desert and drought,
But the rolling words are sea-borne,
The star, a western star
Leading to the mystery
Of the lost lands.

DECEMBER

This translation into Cornish was made by Frances Bennett and appears here with her permission.

MELYAN

NADELAK IN KERNOW

Thew hemma an seson
Lebm'an moar toaz dhan ayr
Ma e anal sellis
Piffia an cregiow
En treven plattia en doar
Mava whetha
Mava crunkia ha thithia
Bedn an penterriow hanadga
Han treathow pell, terrez go asset

Obma ma'n terman tralia gen tedn loor
Mava traynia an leith a dir ma
Bera ha mez an moar
E anal tralia bas ha downe
Carra morienal ha trig an tre'vor

Down en bounderiow calish
Ma'n trevow kidhez gen henwen scant credgez
Cana an howlsedaz podnack
Ha dro than devyth zan zeher
Buz degez gen an moar ew an gerriow rullia
Steran, steran an orlewan
Ledia tha mysteri an terriow kellez

51